CONTENTS

SO-DUV-499

INTRODUCTION

I n the aftermath of World War II, as the tensions of the Cold War grew in the 1950s, the Canadian and United States governments enacted discriminatory policies against LGBTQ+ (lesbian, gay, bisexual, transgender, queer/questioning, and others) workers. Fear of blackmail and bigotry led to the creation of these policies. Potentially thousands of people lost their jobs because of their sexual orientation. The armed forces in both countries enacted policies stating that service members had to choose between being out and staying in the military. People were discharged because of these policies, ending their careers and losing many of their benefits.

Through the end of the 1960s, people could be jailed for committing "homosexual acts." Police would regularly raid bars and clubs looking for LGBTQ+ people breaking decency laws. Until the 1970s, homosexuality (the term used at the time) was considered a mental disorder that could be cured. Laws prohibited same-sex couples from marrying their partners, or from adopting or fostering children. Couples that had been in relationships for decades

The late Harvey Milk became one of the first out elected officials in the United States when he won a seat on the San Francisco Board of Supervisors in 1977.

weren't entitled to the same rights as opposite-sex couples regarding healthcare, pension benefits, and more. LGBTQ+ people now serve in all levels of government in both countries. Lesbian, gay, and bisexual service members are welcome in the military in both the United States and Canada. The Canadian Armed Forces is also open to transgender service members.

Being LGBTQ+ is no longer a crime and no longer treated as a mental disorder. Same-sex couples enjoy marriage equality in both Canada and the United States. Same-sex couples and individuals are gaining their parental rights in both countries. These strides toward equality were made through decades of struggle by activists and allies. Change happened through marches, protests, and boycotts. Change happened through lawsuits, appeals, and Supreme Court decisions. Change happened through the work of individuals, organizations, and communities.

The people behind the fight for LGBTQ+ rights and equality were spurred to action by personal experiences, global injustices, and hope for the future. They stood up against police raids. They organized in the midst of a devastating health crisis. They spoke out for their families. They demanded their right to work, their right to serve, and their right to equal protection under the law. The fight is ongoing. It continues in workplaces

where employers can discriminate against workers based on their sexual orientation or gender
identity. It continues in schools where students
can't access the bathroom or changing room
associated with their gender identity. It continues
in legislatures where discriminatory laws are still
being debated.

Just as with the victories of the past, meeting
these new struggles toward LGBTQ+ equality will
require hard work, engagement, and organization. It will require changes in our communities,
schools, and workplaces. It will require the
efforts of activists and allies standing up and
speaking out against injustice. You will discover
some whose activism made the rights enjoyed
by LGBTQ+ people possible. You will also learn
about the organizations supporting the fight today
and how you can support the cause.

CHAPTER ONE

THE STRUGGLE TO BE SEEN AND HEARD

O n March 7, 1967, the documentary *CBS Reports: The Homosexuals* aired in the United States. The television special featured interviews with gay men and mental health experts and field reports with law enforcement members. One of the gay men, the only one to show his face on camera, was identified as "Warren Adkins." Actually, it was Jack Nichols, an activist and cofounder of the Washington, DC, chapter of the gay rights organization known as the Mattachine Society. In the special, Nichols shared with host Mike Wallace that while his family accepted his sexuality, others he knew had far different experiences. "I had one friend who was beaten savagely by his father, and he beat him in fact with bricks. I was one of the lucky ones, my family reacted, I think, very heroically and humanely," Nichols said.

For the special, CBS commissioned a study by the Opinion Research Corporation to gauge American attitudes toward homosexuals and homosexuality (the commonly used terms of the

Founded in 1950, the Mattachine Society was an early gay activist organization. In 1999, members Bill Reynard, Earl Gebhardt, Rolland Karcher, and Elver Barker were honored during Pride celebrations.

time). The attitudes were overwhelmingly negative. As host Wallace reported, two-thirds of those surveyed viewed homosexuals with disgust, discomfort, or fear. Most surveyed believed that homosexuality was a greater threat to society than adultery, abortion, or prostitution. At that time, homosexuality was considered a mental illness and homosexual acts between consenting adults were a crime in every state but Illinois. Some faced jail time. Others, upon arrest, had their names and addresses published in their local newspaper, which often led to them losing their jobs or being estranged from their families. Employers could freely discriminate against LGBTQ+ workers, either refusing to hire or firing based on an employee's sexual orientation.

During this period in Canada, people lost their jobs and were imprisoned. Some even faced life imprisonment for having consensual same-sex relationships. The law was changed in 1969, but it still took decades for the military to fully integrate and for LGBTQ+ Canadians to be protected from discrimination based on their sexual orientation or gender identity.

Nearly five decades later, a 2017 Pew Research study found that 63 percent of Americans believed that homosexuality (the term used in the survey) should be accepted by society. A 2017 CROP Inc. survey found that 81 percent of LGBT (the term used in the survey) participants believed Canadian society showed a willingness to integrate LGBT communities. That same year, Canadian Prime Minister Justin Trudeau issued a formal apology to the LGBTQ+ community on behalf of the government for the discrimination faced by many Canadians in the twentieth century.

Getting to this place of growing cultural acceptance and legal protections has required decades of struggle from LGBTQ+ people and their allies.

Through acts of civil disobedience and challenges to exclusionary laws, LGBTQ+ Americans and Canadians have continued to demand both their full rights and full place in society.

AN UNWELCOMING SOCIETY

CBS Reports: The Homosexuals featured interviews with three gay men, Nichols appearing as "Warren Adkins" and two other men who wouldn't show their faces on camera. One of the anonymously profiled men was on parole, having been convicted multiple times for lewd acts, and, if caught again, could face life in prison. At the time of the interview, he was undergoing psychiatric treatment.

In the 1950s and 1960s, homosexuality was considered a mental illness that could be cured. Families would send their children to psychiatric hospitals where treatments included aversion therapy, electroshock therapy and, in some cases, lobotomies. Research was happening, though, that would challenge that view. In a study funded by the National Institute of Mental Health, Evelyn Hooker found that gay men were as mentally healthy as heterosexual men. These results were later replicated and eventually led the American Psychiatric Association to remove homosexuality as an illness from its *Diagnostic and Statistical*

Considered to be mentally ill, LGBTQ+ people were sent to psychiatric hospitals to be "cured" in the 1950s. One of the treatments used was electroshock therapy.

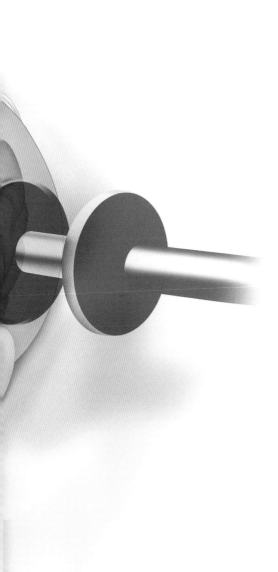

Manual of Mental Disorders, which is the standard classification of mental disorders used by mental health professionals in the United States.

Fear of legal punishment, forced mental health treatments, and job loss meant many LGBTQ+ people of the era kept their sexual orientations and gender identities secret. Some married and started families, keeping their true identities hidden. For those who wanted to live openly, they could join activist and support organizations, known at the time as "homophile" groups, and work

publicly for positive change. One was the Mattachine Society, founded in 1950 by Harry Hay and
Chuck Rowland in Los Angeles. The Mattachine
Society later established chapters around the
United States. Concrete steps in the Silver Lake
neighborhood of Los Angeles, where Hay lived
with his mother, were designated the Mattachine
Society Steps by the Los Angeles City Council
in 2012. Daughters of Bilitis, a lesbian support
network, was founded by Del Martin and Phyllis
Lyon in San Francisco in 1955. When San Francisco Mayor Gavin Newsom sanctioned same-sex
marriages in the city in 2004, Martin and Lyon
were the first couple he wed. There were also
underground gay-friendly establishments where
LGBTQ+ could pursue relationships and develop
a sense of community, from bookstores to bars.
Even these spaces weren't completely safe,
though, and patrons often found themselves subjected to police harassment.

RUN-INS WITH THE LAW

Police regularly raided clubs and bars that catered
to an LGBTQ+ clientele, looking for people who
were violating various decency laws. In New York,
bars could refuse service to disorderly patrons,
and many refused service to LBGTQ+ patrons on

LIVING OPENLY

GLAAD describes coming out as "a lifelong process of self-acceptance." LGBTQ+ people identify first to themselves and then may choose to do so publicly, according to the organization. If someone chooses to identify publicly, coming out doesn't happen just one time, but again and again with each new relationship and acquaintanceship. Because of concerns for acceptance or safety, an LGBTQ+ person may only be out to some of the people in their lives. If a friend chooses to share their sexual orientation or gender identity with you, that does not mean you are free to share their identity with others. The decision of when to come out and to whom is personal and needs to be respected.

Coming out is a powerful tool, according to the Human Rights Campaign (HRC), because if people know someone who is LGBTQ+, they are more likely to support LGBTQ+ equality. Having visible role models is also important to younger LGBTQ+ people. October 11 is National Coming Out Day in the United States and Canada. On this day, LGBTQ+ people, and their allies, celebrate their own coming out and show support to those who are coming out. The day also provides an opportunity to see what work still needs to be done to make the world a safe and accepting place for all LGBTQ+ people.

these grounds, fearing for their liquor licenses. On April 21, 1966, three members of the Mattachine Society staged a protest to challenge this practice of refusing service to LGBTQ+ patrons. The "sip-in" was inspired by the sit-ins organized by civil rights activists at segregated lunch counters. During the protest, the society members, accompanied by reporters, announced their sexual orientation to servers as they placed their orders. Reporters and photographers were there to witness when a bartender at one establishment refused to serve the protesters.

Publicity for the protest gained the attention of the New York City Commission on Human Rights, whose chairman told the *New York Times* that denying service to someone based on their sexual orientation was within the bounds of sex discrimination. The Mattachine Society members later sued bars in New Jersey with the state's Supreme Court ruling that being a homosexual didn't make someone a criminal and that people could not be denied service based on their sexual orientation.

On the other side of the country, as patrons celebrated New Year's 1967 at the Black Cat Tavern in Los Angeles, undercover police arrested couples who were engaging in lewd behavior. They were only hugging and kissing to mark the start of the new year. Two of those arrested had to register as sex offend-

People could be arrested in 1960s New York for wearing clothing associated with the opposite gender. Police raided LGBTQ+ clubs looking for people violating this and other decency laws.

ers. On February 11, more than five hundred people protested the bust in a march organized by Personal Rights in Defense and Education (PRIDE), an activist group founded in 1966. The Black Cat Tavern was designated a Los Angeles Historic-Cultural Monument in 2008 with a plaque identifying it as the "site of the first documented LGBT civil rights demonstration in the nation."

In New York, police were also looking for people who were violating a law dating back to the nineteenth century. The law prohibited a man or woman from wearing the clothing of the opposite sex. As described in the PBS documentary *American Experience: Stonewall Uprising*, during a raid, transgender people or men in drag, as well as those perceived to be wearing clothing of the opposite sex, would be escorted to the bathroom by a female police officer. There, she would confirm their gender. To adhere to the law, men and women had to wear at least three pieces of clothing associated with their sex.

SYMBOLS OF PRIDE

As the gay rights movement grew throughout the 1970s, activists turned to a historical symbol to represent the LGBTQ+ struggle for civil rights. During the Holocaust, gay men were forced to wear pink triangles to identify their sexual orientation. Male same-sex relationships had been against the law in Germany since the 1870s, but that law was strengthened under the Nazis. As a result of enhanced enforcement, five thousand to fifteen thousand men were sent to concentration camps. It's unknown how many of those men died in the camps. The dark history of the pink triangle made it a sadly fitting symbol during the early years of the AIDS crisis when protesters displayed it on signs reading, "Silence = Death."

Seen as criminals, gay men living under Nazi rule were required to wear pink triangles. This symbol of persecution was recast as a symbol of pride in the 1970s.

(continued on the next page)

(continued from the previous page)

A second symbol emerged during this time, one that its maker believed was an important counterbalance to the pink triangle. It was positive and originated within the movement. Army veteran and drag performer Dusty Baker designed a 30-by-50-foot (9-by-15-meter) rainbow flag for the 1978 Gay Freedom Day Parade in San Francisco. Originally, the flag featured eight colorful strips, each with a special significance: hot pink for sex, red for life, orange for healing, yellow for sunlight, green for nature, turquoise for art, indigo for harmony, and violet for spirit. The hot pink was later eliminated, and indigo and turquoise were replaced with a deep blue. One of Baker's rainbow flags, in the three-by-five-foot (.9-by-1.5 meter) size most commonly used today, is in the permanent collection of the Museum of Modern Art in New York City. The White House was lit in the flag's rainbow colors to mark the June 2015 Supreme Court ruling in *Obergefell v. Hodges* that guaranteed the right of same-sex couples to marry across the United States.

DEMANDING A SAFE SPACE

When officers raided the Stonewall Inn in New York City on June 28, 1969, they were looking for patrons violating the clothing law and committing

In June 1969, patrons of New York's Stonewall Inn rose up against police who had raided the establishment. The protest invigorated the gay rights movement around the world.

other lewd acts. The bar attracted LGBTQ+ people from throughout New York, including people who identified as drag queens, street kids, and professionals from a range of industries. Ordinarily, when a bar was raided, patrons would present their IDs and be placed under arrest in an orderly fashion. But as Seymour Pine, deputy assistant in the NYPD morals department, told the makers of *American Experience: Stonewall Uprising,* "This time they said, 'We're not going'." Patrons refused to go into police vehicles as crowds gathered. Soon, there was an uprising on the streets outside the Stonewall, with fires set, police vehicles damaged, and glass broken. Frustrated officers went back into the Stonewall to destroy the bar's interior, witnesses shared in the PBS documentary.

Despite the damage, the bar reopened the next night, attracting larger and larger crowds to protest police mistreatment. A variety of political activist groups were there, including the Black Panthers and anti-war groups. Protests went on for several nights and, though media coverage was limited, the LGBTQ+ community was galvanized. As activist and Stonewall protestor Danny Garvin shared in *American Experience: Stonewall Uprising*: "We had discovered a power that we weren't even aware we had."

Activists were invigorated by Stonewall to do more, like Marsha P. Johnson and Sylvia Rivera, who self-identified as drag queens. Johnson and Rivera started Street Transvestites Action Revolutionaries (STAR) and STAR House in support of homeless transgender youth. A gay liberation march was held to mark the one-year anniversary of the Stonewall Inn raid in the summer of 1970. That march was the catalyst for marches and celebrations that are held throughout the world each June during Pride Month. The Stonewall National Monument was designated in 2016, the first and only LGBTQ+ monument in the United States.

The LGBTQ+ community in Toronto, Ontario, Canada, took to the streets in February 1981, following police raids of four bathhouses in the city that led to the arrests of more than 250 gay men. Not only did three thousand people march through Toronto to protest the police action, but defense funds were started for those who were arrested. The majority of charges were later dropped, according to a CBC report marking the thirty-fifth anniversary of the raids and protest. As Dennis Findlay, president of the Canadian Lesbian and Gay Archives, and participant in the protests, told CBC News: "The outcome of all that was, we became a stronger community, we began to organize, and we learned how to organize really well." Toronto's first pride celebration, held in 1981, grew from these protests. Police Chief Mark Saunders apologized for the raids on behalf of the Toronto Police Services on June 22, 2016, as part of the city's now-annual pride celebrations. The following decades saw the groups and individuals mobilized by these injustices. New generations were inspired by their pioneering work, continuing the fights for justice, equality, and acceptance.

CHAPTER TWO

MATTERS OF LIFE AND DEATH

• •

L GBTQ activists in the 1960s and 1970s were fighting for inclusion, equality, and visibility. The fight in the 1980s took on an even greater significance as the arrival of HIV and AIDS meant many were also fighting for their lives. As theater director George C. Wolfe said in the documentary *Larry Kramer in Love and Anger*, "This horrible disease gave this community a focus that it didn't have, it turned a community into a community, and by sense of community I mean caring for and protecting others."

On July 3, 1981, the *New York Times* published an article by Lawrence K. Altman, "Rare Cancer Seen in 41 Homosexuals," that detailed gay men between the ages of twenty-six and fifty-one in New York and California being diagnosed with Kaposi's sarcoma. This rare cancer was primarily found in men over fifty years old and first appeared as spots on the body. Though the course of Kaposi's sarcoma was previously known to take up to ten years, eight of the men among the reported cases died within twenty-four months of being diagnosed.

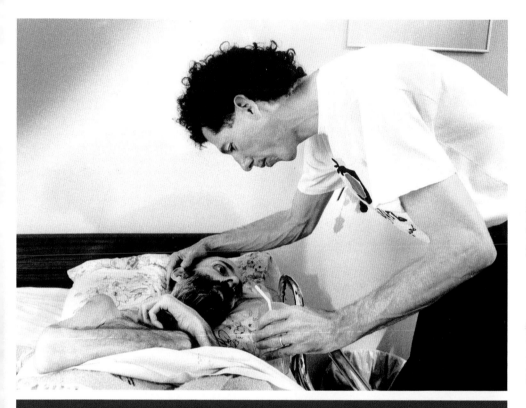

First identified in 1981, AIDS brought new urgency to the struggle for LGBTQ+ rights, with patients fighting discrimination in the workplace, hospitals, and even funeral homes.

A HEALTH CRISIS

By the end of 1981, 121 people had died, with 447 more deaths to follow in 1982, according to the *New York Times*. Doctors and researchers worked to figure out the causes of this immune disorder, which was first referred to as AIDS (acquired immunodeficiency syndrome) on September 24, 1982, by the Centers for Disease Control and Prevention (CDC). With gay men the largest group of diagnosed cases, links were being explored to sexual activity and drug use. As more diagnoses were made, and more deaths occurred, public fear of the disease exposed AIDS patients to discrimination and abuse. Some hospitals refused to treat patients, and some funeral parlors refused to accept remains.

In the early days of the disease, before transmission was understood and HIV (human immunodeficiency virus), the virus that leads to AIDS, was discovered, there was much fear and misinformation surrounding AIDS. We now know HIV is spread only in certain bodily fluids of infected people—blood, semen, preseminal fluid, rectal fluids, vaginal fluids, and breast milk—and mainly through sex or the sharing of needles. However, there was a time when people were afraid of being infected through casual contact like hugging, shaking hands, or sharing a dish with an infected person.

It was in this atmosphere, six years after the publication of the *New York Times* article and with five hundred thousand worldwide AIDS deaths, that ACT UP (AIDS Coalition to Unleash Power) was formed in New York City in 1987. The grassroots organization offered a community of support to people living with AIDS and organized thoughtfully executed protests designed to bring attention to their cause. Lawyers, artists, public relations experts, scientists and other professionals, gay men, lesbians, bisexual and transgender people, and straight allies all brought their skills and expertise to ACT UP. Writer Michael Musto, remembering the people who made up the group, told OUT.com:

> In 1987, when I went to my first meeting of ACT UP—the AIDS activist group [playwright and activist Larry] Kramer cofounded after his split from GMHC [Gay Men's Health Crisis]—I was amazed to see a room without gender barriers. The group furiously brought gay men, lesbians, and others together, all united in the war against the powers-that-be for ignoring the horror of the AIDS epidemic. There wasn't time to second-guess who you were fighting alongside—you just held hands and dove right in, anxious to make a difference.

Peter Staley, a prominent member of ACT UP, and later founder of medical treatment resource AIDSmeds, shared this about the group in the documentary *How to Survive a Plague*:

*To be that threatened with extinction and
to not lay down but instead to stand up
and fight back, the way we did it, the
way we took care of ourselves, and each
other, the goodness that we showed, the
humanity that we showed the world is just
mind-boggling, just incredible.*

ACT UP protested hospitals where AIDS patients
had been physically abused or denied treatment.
The group pressured landlords and public officials
to ensure people wouldn't lose their homes after a
partner died of AIDS. ACT UP protested—and later
worked closely with—government agencies and
drug companies to get new treatments tested. Their
efforts were not just for AIDS, but also for its related
complications, including blindness and pneumonia,
as detailed in the paper "A National AIDS Treatment
Research Agenda" that the group composed and
presented at the Fifth Annual International AIDS
Conference in Montreal in 1989.

As groups including ACT UP were rallying
LGBTQ+ communities in the fight against AIDS,
the scientific community was being mobilized by
amfAR (American Foundation for AIDS Research).
The organization was cofounded in 1985 by scientists and physicians. Among them was Mathilde
Krim, a research scientist who saw the need for
funding to be put into AIDS research. She also put

Legendary actress Elizabeth Taylor used her fame and connections to raise money for AIDS research through amfAR (American Foundation for AIDS Research), an organization she helped found.

her own money toward the cause. Founding international chairman Elizabeth Taylor used her fame
to help the organization raise money that would
be used for research grants and to bring attention
to the health crisis. As the actress told reporters in
an interview shared in the 2013 documentary *The
Battle of amfAR*, "Well I think there are times when
being famous is useful, when it comes in handy,
and if I or any other celebrity can help, then we
should do everything we can. I think that's the only
reason to be famous."

MEMORIALIZING LIVES

In 1987, San Francisco gay rights activists, including Cleve Jones, began making large patchwork
panels to memorialize friends and loved ones
who died from AIDS, in the process launching
the AIDS Memorial Quilt and the NAMES Project
Foundation, the nonprofit custodian of the quilt.
The organization soon received panels from
around the United States, and in October 1987,
the quilt was first displayed on the National Mall
in Washington, DC. It bore 1,920 panels, and was
seen by half a million people, according to the
NAMES Project.

The AIDS Memorial Quilt memorializes people who died from AIDS. The full quilt was last displayed in 1996, but sections are shared at more than one thousand displays annually.

(continued on the next page)

(continued from the previous page)

Each handmade quilt panel measures 3 feet by 6 feet (.9 m by 1.6 m), the size of a human grave, and shares details of lives lost to AIDS in words and pictures. Today, the quilt features more than forty-nine thousand panels, memorializing more than ninety-six thousand individuals, including Marvin Feldman, Jones's friend and the first person to have a panel made for the quilt. The complete quilt hasn't been displayed since 1996, but sections are displayed at the more than one thousand exhibits the NAMES Project Foundation hosts each year.

Lives lost to AIDS are also being remembered on social media through the Instagram account @theaidsmemorial. Inspired by the account's tagline, "What is remembered lives," family members and friends share pictures and memories of the people they lost with the AIDS Memorial's global audience, often on the anniversary of that person's birth or death. The account also shares stories of people who've survived AIDS, thanks to modern-day treatment regimens. The account was started by a Scottish man known only as Stuart. In a *Gay Star News* article, Stuart shared why social media was the ideal venue for this memorial: "I thought Instagram was a perfect way to document the lives of those who had died. I just want more people to hear the stories and remember."

LIVING WITH AIDS

In 1987, AZT became the first drug approved by the CDC to treat AIDS. A welcomed breakthrough, the drug's approval and release wasn't without challenges, with sometimes serious effects and an incredibly high price tag of $10,000 a year. More treatment breakthroughs followed, with AZT still in use, though now part of a drug cocktail regimen. When first introduced in the mid-1990s, this treatment required patients to take sometimes dozens of pills a day. Today, patients take just a few.

These advancements are making it possible for people to live long lives with HIV/AIDS, as Sean Hosein, science and medicine editor for Canadian HIV and hepatitis C information resource CATIE, shared in an article for the organization, "The Evolution of HIV Treatment":

> I remember in the early '90s counselling people on the phone or in person at the CATIE office about their treatment options. In those troubled times it seemed far-fetched that anyone with HIV would ever live to see a day when they could stay healthy, have families and live into old age. Today when I hear HIV-positive people complain about aging-related issues,

Thanks to medical advancements, people have been able to live for decades with HIV/AIDS. Living with the virus means taking combinations of drugs each day.

although I don't say this, on the inside I'm happy for them because they have survived the worst years of the epidemic when so many others did not.

There is still not a cure and new cases continue to be diagnosed. According to the CDC, there were 39,782 new diagnoses in the United States in 2016 (the most current numbers available). The government of Canada estimated 2,570 new HIV cases in 2014 (the most current numbers available). Gay and bisexual men, and transgender women, are among the groups at highest risk for infection, a statistic that has prohibited men who have sex with men (MSM) from donating blood.

Following the discovery of HIV transmission through a blood transfusion, procedures were put in place to safeguard the blood supply, including testing and comprehensive questionnaires given to potential donors. MSM were seen as a high-risk group, and soon regulations were put in place to prevent these men from donating blood. In 1992, a Health Canada regulation was enacted prohibiting all men who had sex with a man, even just once, since 1977 from donating blood. The United States enacted a similar lifetime ban for MSM.

Testing advancements led to reviews of these policies. In 2013, the ineligibility period in Canada was reduced to five years and later one year. The United States also now has a one-year ineligibility period. This still prohibits sexually active MSM from donating blood, regardless of number of partners or other risk factors, a prohibition that led Toronto-area gay rights activist Christopher Karas to file a human rights complaint in 2016 alleging the ban was discriminatory. Paralegal James Hill explained Karas's argument to the CBC in a interview: "If you're going to have a one-year wait, just apply it across the board to everybody or get rid of it entirely. It's discriminatory to base this on sexual orientation."

PEDRO ZAMORA'S EDUCATIONAL CRUSADE

For a few months in 1994, MTV viewers got to experience life as an HIV-positive person, thanks to the third season of *The Real World* and cast member Pedro Zamora, a twenty-two-year-old gay man who'd been diagnosed with HIV at age seventeen. Soon after his diagnosis, Zamora became an HIV education advocate in his native Florida, speaking at churches, schools, and even to Congress. Reality TV, though, presented his largest platform.

On camera, Zamora shared a scrapbook detailing his advocacy work. He took his roommates to his speeches and educated them about HIV. As an educator, Zamora spoke honestly about being infected through unprotected sex and urged young people to practice safe sex. Sharing this information was vital, as Zamora shared in his July 12, 1994, congressional testimony: "What we need is the collective will to care about young people and about people with different backgrounds and make sure that one day people grow up in a world without AIDS."

He also shared his personal life, including his relationship with activist Sean Sasser. Their commitment ceremony was shown on *The Real World*.

(continued on the next page)

(continued from the previous page)

Zamora's health declined during his time on *The Real World*. After filming wrapped, he developed PML (progressive multifocal leukoencephalopathy), a disease that attacked the frontal lobe of his brain, causing Zamora to lose the ability to speak. He died on November 11, 1994, hours after the season finale of *The Real World* aired.

The late activist and health educator Pedro Zamora (*left*) gained national attention as a cast member on MTV's *The Real World*. He used the show to educate viewers about HIV.

US president Bill Clinton released this statement after Zamora's death was announced: "Through his work with MTV, he taught young people that 'The Real World' includes AIDS and that each of us has the responsibility to protect ourselves and our loved ones."

EDUCATION AS PREVENTION

While work continues to find a cure, discoveries have been made to improve prevention. People who don't have HIV but are at risk have options to protect themselves, including through safer sex, regular testing, PrEP, and PEP. PrEP (pre-exposure prophylaxis) are medicines taken every day before possible exposure, including through sex with someone who is HIV positive or has an unknown HIV status. According to the National Institutes of Health (NIH), PrEP can reduce risk of getting HIV through sex by more than 90 percent. PEP (post-exposure prophylaxis) is taken within seventy-two hours of possible exposure. The NIH warns, though, that PEP can prevent infection when taken correctly but that it is not always effective.

Sharing information about prevention methods like PrEP and PEP, as well as safer sex, are essential to reduce infection rates. School sex

People at high risk of contracting HIV can use medications known as PrEP (pre-exposure prophylaxis) to lower their risk of infection.

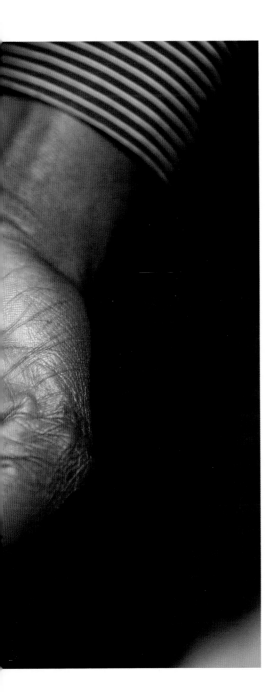

education programs are an ideal venue for this information, but many are lacking, particularly in providing sexual health information to LGBTQ+ students. In the United States, sex education curricula ranges from comprehensive, offering students information on contraception and sexually transmitted infection (STI) prevention, to abstinence only, with students taught that sex is appropriate only within heterosexual marriage. Meanwhile in Canada, LGBTQ+-inclusive curricula are being proposed and enacted.

There are consequences if people don't have access to accurate, comprehensive information about their sexual health. Though not a risk group for HIV, queer women are at risk for other STIs, as Cathy Sakimura, deputy director of the National Center for Lesbian Rights, told *Newsweek* in "Schools Won't Teach Children About Lesbian Sex and That's Hurting Queer Girls": "Studies show that young queer women have higher rates of teen pregnancy and STIs. And hetero-centric sex ed goes into that." Groups including legal organization Lambda Legal are working with students, educators, and community members to speak out against exclusionary curriculum and improve education for all students.

CHAPTER THREE

AN INCLUSIVE AND SAFE LEARNING ENVIRONMENT

C hildren in the United States and Canada all have the right to a free public education. Though entitled to attend, not all students find school a secure and welcoming place. In its 2017 report "Violence and LGBTQ Communities: What We Do Know, and What Do We Need to Know?," research firm RTI International found, "Sexual minority youth are more likely than heterosexual youth to be victims of bullying and bias-related victimization, based on strong and consistent evidence across many large studies."

In addition to bullying, students may also face discrimination when it comes to clubs they want to join, sports team they'd like to play for, or events they'd like to attend. School lessons may also be problematic when students don't see their lives and experiences reflected in what is being taught in the classroom. Or, they may not get a complete health education because of their sexual orientation or gender identity.

Instituting more inclusive policies at schools would have a variety of benefits. Amanda

LGBTQ+ students face bullying and discrimination at higher rates than other students. Antidiscrimination laws, inclusive curricula, and a supportive environment can improve school life for LGBTQ+ students.

Guthrie, education and operations manager with community center OUTSaskatoon, explained to CBC News that if we don't talk about individuals' identities, then society's norms that "people are or should be heterosexual and cisgender" are only reinforced. Guthrie continues: "So, if we simply talk about the lived realities and that LGBT people have always existed then we are going to be making safer spaces and normalizing LGBT identities."

LESSONS IN REPRESENTATION

Parents, students, educators, and activists in Canada and the United States are working to see that LGBTQ+ students, and students with LGBTQ+ family members, feel included and represented by their classroom curriculum. Suits have been filed and laws passed to ensure that the stories, contributions, and lives of LGBTQ+ people have a place in schools, which would have benefits for all students, proponents say.

Attorney Allison Fenske with the Public Interest Law Centre in Winnipeg is representing families who filed discrimination complaints with the Manitoba Human Rights Commission regarding noninclusive curriculum. Fenske told CBC News that the issue wasn't so much about people's sexuality or their gender identity. It was more "about family diversity and understanding and accepting everyone. And so students have to be able to see themselves and their families reflected in their school and know that their families matter."

Students in California are learning about the contributions of LGBTQ+ people in their social studies books. Introduced by Senator Mark Leno in 2010 and signed into law in by Governor Jerry Brown on July 14, 2011, the state's FAIR Education Act requires that history and social studies curriculum include fair, accurate, inclusive, and respectful references to the contributions of people with disabilities and LGBT (the term used in the act) people. Under the act, students can learn about historical figures and events, stereotypes, self-expression, and allyship, among a wide range of other topics.

Other states, though, have passed laws to make curriculum less inclusive. Civil rights organization Lambda Legal tracks restrictive laws from eight states through #donteraseus: A Campaign to End Anti-LGBT Curriculum Laws. Lambda Legal is organizing students, educators, and community members to speak out against these laws. Though designed to specifically address sex education, these laws can be applied more broadly to all curriculum, as Lambda Legal explains on its website:

> These laws have a chilling effect on LGBT-inclusive curriculum, programs, and policies, even where they would not actually bc barred by these laws. In other words, even where these laws do not prohibit teaching about gay civil rights leader Harvey Milk in a history class or reading a Walt Whitman poem in an English class, schools and teachers may misinterpret

them as doing so. That uniquely harms LGBT students, but it also deprives other students of the benefits of an accurate, inclusive education.

WELCOMED AT PROM

Aniya Wolf was turned away from prom at Bishop McDevitt High School in Harrisburg, Pennsylvania, for wearing a tuxedo. The school said she violated its dress code policy. Paula Goodgame couldn't bring her girlfriend to her prom at St. Petersburg Catholic High School in St. Petersburg, Florida, because the school wouldn't allow students to bring same-sex dates to dances. Stories like these made national headlines and raised questions about what rights LGBTQ+ students have when it comes to wearing what they want and bringing who they want to their high school proms. The American Civil Liberties Union (ACLU) published the guide, "Know Your Prom Night Rights!" which explains that courts have ruled in favor of public school students who want to attend prom with their desired date, regardless of gender, and of female students who want to wear a tux.

In Canada, high schooler Marc Hall sued the Durham Catholic School District Board to be able to take his boyfriend to prom in 2002. An injunction was granted that enabled the couple to go, but Hall dropped the case three years later. Hall's story inspired a made-for-TV movie and a musical. Private religious schools may not have to follow the same guidelines, though. Organizations, including the ACLU and Lambda Legal, provide resources and assistance to LGBTQ+ students facing discrimination at prom.

Aniya Wolf (*left*) was barred from prom for wearing a suit rather than a dress. Students have fought to attend prom in the clothing and with the date of their choice.

RIGHTS AND PROTECTIONS

Mack Beggs won back-to-back Texas state wrestling championships in the girls' division. Despite beginning his transition from female to male, and taking tes-tosterone, Beggs was not permitted to wrestle in boys' division during high school. This was because of a provision by the governing University Interscholastic League requiring student ath-letes to compete under the gender listed on their birth certificate. This decision, unpopular with Beggs's supporters and opponents on the wres-tling mat, led to lawsuits and national media atten-tion. Yet all high schooler Beggs wanted to do is wrestle in the boys' divi-

Though transitioning from female to male, Mack Beggs was not allowed to join the boys' wrestling team at his high school and had to continue to wrestle on the girls' team.

sion, an opportunity he would eventually have once he entered college. Before his college plans were setlled, the athlete shared during a *Star-Tele-gram* interview: "I'm looking forward to college, I'm looking forward to being on a men's team, being in the men's division, working on my takedowns, being as strong as the guys. I'm already a couple of years behind, so I have a lot to catch up on."

When Beggs graduated from high school in June 2018, he had good news. Life University. located in Marietta Georgia, had offered him a wrestling scholarship—and he would compete on the men's team.

LGBTQ+ students like Beggs are standing up By and speaking out for fair treatment and equal rights in school. In addition to the challenges all teenagers face, students may also have to con-tend with not being able to use the bathroom, dress in the uniform, or play on the sports team related to their gender identity. They may not be able to bring their boyfriend or girlfriend to prom. They may not get permission to start LGBTQ+ clubs on campus.

Students in the United States are protected by the Constitution and a range of federal and state laws, including Title IX. This federal law, which applies to kindergarten through high school facili-ties and colleges receiving federal funding, states: "No person in the United States shall, on the basis of sex, be excluded from participation in, be denied the benefits of, or be subjected to discrimination under any education program or activity receiving Federal financial assistance." According to Lambda Legal, courts made sure that these protections were also granted to LGBTQ+ individuals targeted by sex discrimination or harassment.

Thanks to this patchwork of protections, LGBTQ+ public school students in the United States should have their personal information protected, including transgender status and health information. They should also be able to exercise free speech regarding LGBTQ+ issues and attend school free from harassment and discrimination. Not every state, though, offers students the same protections, and private schools may not have to adhere to the same regulations and restrictions. Whether you attend public or private school, regardless of the state, there are local and national organizations that can assist if you believe your rights are being violated.

Students in Canada are protected by the Canadian Charter of Rights and Freedoms, as well as federal, provincial, and territorial laws. This includes the Canadian Human Rights Act, which was updated in June 19, 2017, through the passage of Bill C-16 to include gender identity and gender expression on its list of prohibited grounds of discrimination. Part 1 of the act reads:

The fight continues for transgender students to be able to use the bathroom and changing room of their choice. Some schools offer students the option of using a gender-neutral bathroom.

For all purposes of this Act, the prohibited grounds of discrimination are race, national or ethnic origin, colour, religion, age, sex, sexual orientation, gender identity or expression, marital status, family status, genetic characteristics, disability and conviction for an offence for which a pardon has been granted or in respect of which a record suspension has been ordered.

SUPPORTING LGBTQ+ TEENS IN CRISIS

In 1995, producers Peggy Rajski and Roger Stone accepted an Academy Award for their short film *Trevor*. It tells the story of a thirteen-year-old boy who attempts suicide after his classmates learned he was gay. As they promoted the film, the filmmakers discovered how few resources existed for LGBTQ+ teens like Trevor. They then launched the Trevor Project, a crisis intervention and suicide prevention organization.

When accepting the Academy Award on March 27, 1995, Rajski talked about the inspiration for the film:

> *Well, Trevor first came to life as a stage piece conceived after our wonderful writer James Lecesne heard a report on NPR about teen suicide and learned that approximately one-third of all teens who kill themselves are gay. We made our film for anyone who's ever felt like an outsider. It celebrates all those who make it through difficult times and mourns those who didn't.*

Among the free services offered by the Trevor Project are a 24/7 crisis line, a confidential instant messaging service, and a confidential texting service. The organization also offers training for

(continued on the next page)

(continued from the previous page)

students, faculty, and staff. According to its 2016 annual report, more than two hundred thousand youth are impacted by the Trevor Project's programs each year.

With these protections, students should be able to attend school without fear of discrimination. They should be able to protect their personal information, including their gender identity and sexual orientation. Students should be free to form LGBTQ+ school organizations. Students should be able to access the washroom, locker room, or other space that corresponds to their gender identity. If you feel your rights have been violated at school, there are local and national organizations to turn to for support, as well as your province's Human Rights Commission.

HEALTHY AND SAFE

In addition to sometimes struggling for fairness in school, far too many LGBTQ+ students are also dealing with bullying or violence. According to the study "Being Safe, Being Me: Results of the Canadian Trans Youth Health Survey" released by the University of British Columbia in 2017, 55 percent of younger survey participants reported being bullied once or more in the past year. Thirteen percent said they'd been bullied twelve times or more. Of younger participants, 64 percent reported that they had been taunted or ridiculed, and 36 percent had been physically threatened or injured.

The CDC learned about LGB bullying in its "2015 Youth Risk Behavior Survey." According to the survey, 10 percent of participants were threatened or injured with a weapon on school property, and 34 percent were bullied on school property. By comparison, just over 5 percent of heterosexual participants reported being threatened or injured with a weapon on school property, and just under 19 percent reported being bullied on school property.

Feeling unsafe can lead some students to skip school. As reported in the "Youth Risk Behavior Survey," LGB students were 140 percent more likely than heterosexual students to have not gone to school one or more days in the previous thirty days because of safety concerns. Because of a variety of factors, LGB youth are at greater risk for depression, suicide, and substance abuse, according to the CDC.

Support can make a difference. CDC research found that LGB students at schools with groups like gay-straight alliances were less likely to face threats of violence, take time off from school because they felt unsafe, or attempt suicide than

Allies can make a big difference in stopping the bullying of LGBTQ+ students at school. Gay-straight alliances (GSAs) are one way to create a welcoming and safe campus for all students.

students whose schools didn't have those support groups. All students, LGBTQ+ and allies, have the right to form supportive groups on campus.

The internet can also provide resources and support to young LGBTQ+ people and their friends. Inspired by a short film set in the 1980s about a gay teenager who attempts suicide, the Trevor Project provides phone, text, and chat crisis intervention and suicide prevention services to LGBTQ+ teens and young adults. In his online introduction to the film *Trevor*, YouTuber Tyler Oakley said of the film:

> *Of course we know that Trevor's story doesn't reflect every young person's reality, and times have definitely changed since the 1980s, however the message of the film holds true, everyone, regardless of who you love or what your gender identity is, deserves to have a future and feel like their life matters.*

That message fits the organization, as well.

The It Gets Better Project aims to uplift, empower, and connect young LGBTQ+ people through educational programs, outreach efforts, and connections to supportive services in more than thirty countries. Launched as a social media campaign in 2010 by Dan Savage and husband, Terry Miller, the organization has shared over sixty thousand videos from LGBTQ+ people and allies to let those watching know they're not alone.

CHAPTER FOUR

OUT IN THE WORKPLACE

O n January 9, 2017, US secretary of state John Kerry issued an apology on behalf of the State Department to LGBTQ+ employees and activists who had faced discrimination from the agency. Secretary Kerry wrote:

> In the past—as far back as the 1940s, but continuing for decades—the Department of State was among many public and private employers that discriminated against employees and job applicants on the basis of perceived sexual orientation, forcing some employees to resign or refusing to hire certain applicants in the first place. These actions were wrong then, just as they would be wrong today.

LGBTQ+ government and private-sector employees and applicants in the United States and Canada have long faced workplace discrimination. In the 1940s and 1950s, the State Department fired gay employees, which laid the groundwork for President Dwight D. Eisenhower's Executive Order 10450 in 1953. It banned gay men and lesbians from working in the federal government (it would take more than sixty years for the executive order to be fully repealed). Because of laws at the time barring same-sex relationships and what were then deemed "homosexual acts," some employees feared LGBTQ+ workers would be susceptible to blackmail. Others were driven to discriminate by prejudice. As a result, some people lost their jobs. Others weren't hired. This era of discrimination against LGBTQ+ employees in the government became known as the Lavender Scare.

On November 28, 2017, Canadian prime minister Trudeau issued an apology on his country's behalf to LGBTQ+ government workers and military personnel during a period that's become known as the LGBT Purge. Delivering his remarks in the House of Commons, the prime minister said:

> *Today, we finally talk about Canada's role in the systemic oppression, crim inalization, and violence against the lesbian, gay, bisexual, transgender, queer, and two-spirit communities. And it is my hope that in talking about these injustices, vowing to never repeat them,*

Prime Minister Justin Trudeau marched in the 2016 Vancouver Pride Parade. In 2017, he issued an apology on behalf of the government to LGBTQ+ Canadians who experienced workplace discrimination.

and acting to right these wrongs, we can begin to heal.

AN ONGOING STRUGGLE

Even as these apologies were being issued, LGBTQ+ people continued to face discrimination in the workplace. According to "LGBT Realities," a 2017 survey of LGBT Canadians (the term used in the survey results) commissioned by the Fondation Jasmin Roy, an organization that fights discrimination, bullying, and violence against children in schools, 33 percent of respondents reported experiencing bullying, threats, or hurtful or derogatory comments at work. Forty percent of those surveyed experienced discrimination in the workplace. Twenty-one percent reported being either fired, forced to quit, or not hired because of their gender identity or sexual orientation.

The 2017 "Working for Inclusion Report" from the US Commission on Human Rights found that employers had a less favorable reaction to employees perceived to be LGBT (the term used in the report). It also found that those applicants got around 30 percent fewer callbacks for jobs than other applicants. The commission also found reported incidences across the country of LGBT workers losing their jobs because of discrimination. Of this discrimination, the commission wrote: "Such discriminiation persists and has wide-ranging, damaging implications for the quality of life for many LGBT Americans, their children and families, and communities."

LGBTQ+ workers in both countries continue to face discrimination, despite laws being in place that are supposed to protect all workers. In the United States, though, the level of protection a worker has depends on where they live. Workplace legal protections, much like for students, can also differ whether you work for a government agency or private employer. Advocacy organizations including Lambda Legal and the HRC track state and local laws that impact LGBTQ+ workers and provide helpful resources for these workers.

Resources like these can help LGBTQ+ workers protect their rights. Resources also exist to help LGBTQ+ workers find fair and welcoming employers to work for and allies to find the companies they'd like to support as consumers. HRC releases the "Corporate Equality Index" every year that rates workplaces on LGBTQ equality (the term used in the index). The annual list of "Canada's Best Diversity Employers" from Mediacorp recognizes employers for their workplace diversity and inclusiveness programs for groups including LGBTQ workers (the term used in the list). There are also online job boards and recruitment sites that offer their own listings of LGBQT+ friendly employers.

Some companies, including a few ranked highly by the HRC, have begun keeping data on their employees' gender identity and sexual orientation. As reported by *Bloomberg* in 2016, large corporations in the United States, including Facebook and AT&T, were asking employees if they'd like to disclose this information. The input would then be used to help craft more inclusive benefits plans and diversity programming. Having potentially faced bullying, discrimination, or even job loss, some LGBTQ+ workers may choose not to come out at work, though. The decision to come out at work is a personal one that should be respected, as Kathy Tu, cohost of the *Nancy* podcast, shared with *Vice*:

> *People should come out if they feel safe doing so. You should feel no pressure. Until then, you've got to feel out what's good for you. I don't think there's a need to push yourself to do something that could put you in a dangerous situation. You have to listen to your gut on this.*

BUYING POWER

One way you can support LGBTQ+ rights and causes is with your wallet. This can include making purchases from companies that embrace inclusion in their employee policies, customer service, and even advertising and avoiding companies that discriminate. Your purchases can send a powerful message, as the HRC explains in its online Buyers Guide:

Whether you are buying a cup of coffee or renovating your home, by supporting businesses that support workplace equality you send a powerful message that LGBTQ inclusion is good for the bottom line.

If your family's making travel plans, you can choose to visit regions that protect LGBTQ+ rights and skip places with discriminatory laws. When the North Carolina legislature passed House Bill 2 (HB2) in 2016, a law that in part required people to use the bathroom and locker room associated with the gender on their birth certificate, the state quickly faced an economic backlash. Companies chose not to expand their businesses in the state. Conventions, sporting events, and concerts were cancelled. Tourists chose not to visit North Carolina. In part because of its economic effects, the bill has since been replaced with House Bill 142 in 2017, though advocates caution it's not fully repealed.

If you're unsure of a company's policies or record regarding LGBTQ+ rights, a number of organizations, including the HRC, offer guides that can help allies choose the companies they will support with their wallets. These organizations can also provide information on discriminatory laws that you can reference before your next family trip.

(continued on the next page)

(continued from the previous page)

Allies can use their purchasing power to support LGBTQ+ people and causes by buying from inclusive companies and boycotting those with discriminatory policies.

WORKPLACE RIGHTS AND PROTECTIONS

The Canadian Human Rights Act prohibits discrimination based on grounds including sex, sexual orientation, gender identity, and gender expression. Under the act, employers are prohibited from treating LGBTQ+ employees differently than other employees in areas including hiring, promotions, training, and firing. Employees who believe they've faced discrimination can contact their provincial Human Rights Commission.

Workers in the United States are protected by federal, state, and local laws. One of these laws is Title VII of the Civil Rights Act of 1964. It bans employment discrimination that is based on sex, race, color, religion, or national origin. As Lambda Legal explains:

> *While there is currently no federal statute that uses the terms "sexual orientation" and "gender identity" to describe prohibited discrimination in private-sector (nongovernment) jobs, transgender workers have had widespread success invoking the prohibition of sex discrimination in Title VII of the Civil Rights Act of 1964. And lesbian, gay, and bisexual workers are increasingly able to invoke Title VII as well.*

Title VII also called for the creation of the US Equal Employment Opportunity Commission (EEOC), which enforces federal employment discrimination laws and covers most employers in the United States with fifteen or more employees. State and local laws can protect employees at smaller companies. Laws on the state and local level can also strengthen federal protections. One example of this shared by Lambda Legal is in states that protect workers based on their perceived sexual orientation and gender identity. This means even if a worker isn't LGBTQ+, or hasn't shared their sexual orientation or gender identity at work, but is discriminated against, they will be protected by the law.

These extra protections don't exist in all states and localities, though. There are seventeen states that have no protections for employees on the basis of sexual orientation, gender identity, or gender expression, including North Carolina, a state that made headlines and faced an economic boycott thanks to the passage of HB2, a law that barred local jurisdictions from passing LGBTQ+ protections. Workers in these states can turn to organizations, including Lambda Legal and the ACLU, for assistance in fighting for equal protections wherever they work.

THE RIGHT TO SERVE

From 1976 to 1988, lesbian, gay, and bisexual troops couldn't serve openly in the Canadian Armed Forces. This was because of Canadian Forces Administrative Order (CFAO) 19-20,

IN SUPPORT OF LGBTQ+ SERVICE MEMBERS

When the law banning lesbian, gay, and bisexual Americans from serving openly in the military was repealed in September 20, 2011, the fight for equal treatment was far from over. At the time of the repeal, the tens of thousands of service members who'd been discharged under the law known as "Don't Ask, Don't Tell" didn't automatically get their discharges upgraded to honorable. As a result, they weren't eligible for some military benefits. Same-sex military spouses weren't guaranteed the same access to benefits as all other military spouses. Transgender Americans were still banned from serving at the time of the repeal, and their place in the US military remains in question.

LGBTQ+ military support and advocacy groups continue working on behalf of active-duty and veteran service members and their families to achieve full quality. OutServe-SLDN is a legal advocacy group representing LGBT (the term used by the organization) service members and veterans with issues, including working to have discharge paperwork upgraded for those impacted by "Don't Ask, Don't Tell."

The American Military Partner Association (AMPA) provides resources and support to the

(continued on the next page)

(continued from the previous page)

partners, spouses, families, and allies of LGBT (the term used by the organization) service members. It has pursued legal action on behalf of same-sex partners of service members. AMPA pitches stories about the families it represents to media outlets around the country to educate the public about the specific challenges they face. It also hosts events that bring the families of LGBT service members together, in addition to other programs and services.

The right of transgender Americans to serve in the military remains in question. The Canadian military has fully welcomed LGBTQ+ service-members since 2012.

SPARTA is a membership organization for LGBT (the term used by the organization) people who are currently serving in the military, as well as veterans, families, and allies. The group advocates for equal treatment of all service members through networking, peer support, educational outreach, and policy advocacy.

Homosexuality—Sexual Abnormality Investigation, Medical Examination and Disposal. Beginning in 1992, those who did serve could choose to continue to do so, but would face career restrictions because of their sexual orientation. The ban was revoked in 1992, thanks to a court case brought by discharged service member Michelle Douglas.

Douglas was appointed to a special unit investigating the sexual orientations of members of the Canadian forces. Within weeks of joining the unit, Douglas herself was being investigated. She was interrogated for two days about her personal life and was asked to speculate on the sexual orientation of other service members. Douglas eventually told investigators she was gay and was discharged in 1989. She took the military to court, and her case led the Federal Court of Canada to order the Canadian Armed Forces to end its discriminatory policies. Douglas was awarded a

Michelle Douglas (*left*) was discharged from the Canadian military in 1989 because of her sexual orientation. Her lawsuit challenging the discriminatory policy helped open military service to LGBTQ+ Canadians.

settlement, but her military career was over.

Michelle Douglas told the *Globe and Mail*: "I should have had a distinguished career path in the military. Instead, on bald discrimination, this was the basis for my dismissal. It's just shocking."

The Canadian military now enjoys a global reputation for inclusion, thanks to the 1992 action and a 2012 policy protecting transgender service members. Work remains to be done for LGBTQ+ service members to enjoy full inclusion in the US military.

On July 19, 1993, President

Shane Ortega served in both the US Army and Marine Corps. The self-described two-spirit veteran advocates for equal protection for LGBTQ+ servicemembers.

Clinton announced the policy known as "Don't Ask, Don't Tell." It prohibited LBGTQ+ people from serving openly in the military. The policy led to the discharge of more than thirteen thousand people, according to the Williams Institute at the University of California Los Angeles School of Law, and was opposed by civil rights organizations, advocacy groups, and the American Psychological Association (APA). Those who were discharged under "Don't Ask, Don't Tell" lost their careers and benefits. Those who stayed in the military feared getting caught, as Shane Ortega, a self-described two-spirit US Army and Marine Corps veteran, shared in the 2016 documentary *The Trans List*:

> *When I went into the United States Marine Corps, it was still under "Don't Ask, Don't Tell." I think that my recruiter thought I was a lesbian and so he made me sign the waiver that says I'm not a homosexual or whatever, but he gave me this odd look when I was signing it. I definitely felt the oppression, as far as it applies to my sexuality, I identify as queer pansexual, for me it was kind of a sense of panic, it's like a witch hunt, someone is going to jump out of the woods like, "Ah! Got you!"*

"Don't Ask, Don't Tell" was repealed by President Barack Obama in 2011. Not only are lesbian, gay, and bisexual service members allowed to serve openly, but their family members are entitled to the same benefits as all other military families. Service members discharged under the policy, as well as those discharged in the decades prior, can apply to have their discharges upgraded and regain their full benefits.

Helen Grace James was discharged from the Air Force in 1955, and at the age of ninety, successfully sued for an upgrade in 2018. Following the ruling, she told NBC News in an interview, "The Air Force recognizes me as a full person in the military."

In 2016, the Obama administration announced a plan that would allow transgender recruits to join the armed services starting in 2018. However, a newly sworn in President Trump issued an order in July 2017 banning transgender soldiers from serving in the military. The backlash was swift: Civil rights groups sued on grounds that the ban was unconstitutional, and federal judges struck it down. However, as of late 2018. transgender recruits eager to enlist are still waiting. SPARTA, an organization for transgender recruits, troops, and veterans, says that out of its 140 members who are trying to enlist, only two have made it into the service since January 1st.

As politicians at all levels seek to retract hard-won legal protections for the LGBTQ community in and out of the military, the reaction is hard to ignore. While record numbers of minorities are running in the Democratic party, the number of LGBTQ candidates has started to swell as well. Known as the "rainbow wave," 430 openly gay, lesbian, bisexual, or transgender citizens have stepped up to run for office in 2018, according to Jessica Taylor of National Public Radio. Regardless of the outcome of these elections, clearly the American political system is headed for change.

CHAPTER FIVE

MATTERS OF LOVE AND FAMILY

W riter and activist Dan Savage remembered the homophobic views he heard from his father when he was growing up in Chicago in the 1970s. He shares the following in an episode of the *WTF with Marc Maron* podcast:

> *That was his argument, we were a threat to the economy because gay people didn't settle down, in his experience gay people, they didn't get married, they didn't have families, so they didn't buy cars and houses and washing machines, and so GE would run out of money and the economy would collapse, that was his theory. And, of course, we didn't get married or have families because you wouldn't let us, as opposed to we didn't want to, we wanted to, but we couldn't.*

American author and activist Dan Savage first married his husband, Terry Miller, in Canada in 2005. The couple was able to marry in the United States seven years later.

That economic argument didn't hold. Both Canada and the United States have seen economic benefits from legalizing same-sex marriage. One example is found in weddings. In 2013, RateSupermarket.ca estimated a potential economic contribution of $566,585,415 (Canadian) from the weddings that had occurred since same-sex marriage was legalized in the country in 2005. In 2016, one year after the *Obergefell v. Hodges* Supreme Court decision that legalized same-sex marriage in the United States, the Williams Institute at the University of California School of Law gave an estimated $1.58 billion (USD) boost to state and local economies, and $102 million (USD) in estimated state and local sales tax revenue.

The couples who've been able to marry have experienced economic benefits, too, including spouses being covered on each other's health insurance, the ability to move to another state for work without worrying about losing their legal relationship status, and knowing that spouses are eligible to receive Social Security and other benefits. There are far more personal benefits, too, of having relationships legally recognized, which is why same-sex couples in both Canada and the United States fought so long and hard for marriage equality.

BEING AN ALLY IN ELECTIONS

By voting in all local, state, and national elections, you can support the issues you care most about, including battling LGBTQ+ discrimination. Your vote can impact laws governing school curriculum, the workplace, healthcare, and family rights. In Canada, citizens who will be age eighteen or older on Election Day and are registered to vote can vote in elections. In the United States, voting is open to citizens age eighteen or older, though states can restrict those rights for people convicted of a felony.

Turnout by younger voters is lower than that of other age groups. According to data from Elections Canada, the 2011 Canadian General Elections saw just under 39 percent of voters eighteen to twenty-four turn out to vote, the lowest turnout of any age group. Despite that number jumping up to slightly over 57 percent in the 2015 general election, this age group still has the lowest turnout. Groups, including Apathy Is Boring and Student Vote, are working in schools and communities to get students excited about voting and engage the next generation of voters.

Data from the US Election Project showed an increase in turnout of voters age eighteen to twenty-four between the 2012 and 2016 presidential elections, growing from just under 41 percent to just over 43 percent. Like young voters in Canada, voter turnout for this age group was the lowest. Groups including Rock the Vote provide registration resources and voting guides for young voters. They also advocate on the state level to make registering and voting simpler, such as enabling people to register to vote when they get their driver's licenses and instituting vote-by-mail in every state. Registering is the first step. Staying up-to-date on current issues, proposed legislation, and candidate platforms will make you an informed voter ready for Election Day.

THE RIGHT TO MARRY

Jim Egan and Jack Nesbit had been together for nearly forty years, sharing a home and bank account, and running a business in British Columbia. A year after Egan retired and began collecting his federal pension, he applied to have spousal benefits granted to Nesbit. The application was denied because, at that time, Canadian law limited marriage rights to opposite-sex couples. Egan and Nesbit appealed the denial, first in federal

Jim Egan (*in the vehicle, on the left*) and Jack Nesbit (*on the right*) fought to have same-sex couples granted the same rights and protections as opposite-sex couples in Canada.

court, then in federal appeals court, and finally on to the Canadian Supreme Court in 1995.

Ahead of the Supreme Court ruling, Svend Robinson, the first out member of Parliament, told the *Washington Post*:

If Jim and Jack win, all federal statutes will have to be reviewed to be sure they don't discriminate. The highest court in the land will be sending a message that lesbian and gay relationships are to be realized as equal to common-law relationships in Canadian society.

The couple lost each of the appeals, but their lawsuits helped pave the way for same-sex marriages to be recognized in Canada.

In 1996, The Canadian Human Rights Act was amended to include sexual orientation as a prohibited ground for discrimination via the passage of Bill C-33. Same-sex couples were granted the same social and tax benefits as opposite-sex couples in common-law relationships via Bill C-23, assented in 2000. Over the next few years, court cases were heard challenging the legality of limiting marriage to opposite-sex couples, and individual provinces began recognizing same-sex marriages, beginning with Ontario in 2003.

Same-sex marriage was legalized in Canada on July 20, 2005, via Bill C-38, making it the fourth country in the world to recognize same-sex marriages. Under the law, married same-sex couples were entitled to the same benefits and protections as opposite-sex couples. Same-sex common-law relationships would also have the same benefits and protections as those enjoyed by opposite-sex couples. Transgender spouses would also enjoy the same protections and benefits. Following the law's enactment, thousands of same-sex couples from around the world came to Canada to get married, including many from the United States ahead of the country's own embrace of marriage embrace.

Edith Windsor (*depicted on the right in the sign*) challenged discrimination against same-sex couples in the United States following the death of her wife, Thea Spyer (*depicted on the left*).

Edith Windsor and Thea Spyer were one of those American couples. Together more than forty years, the two travelled to Canada in 2007 to wed as Spyer battled multiple sclerosis. Spyer died within two years of the wedding, and Windsor got a large tax bill from the federal government. She decided to challenge the bill, and her challenge ended up in the Supreme Court. Windsor said of the tax bill in a 2013 statement shared on NPR: "On a practical level, due to DOMA, I was taxed $363,000 in federal estate tax that I would not have had to pay if I had been married to man named Theo."

The case *United States v. Windsor* challenged the constitutionality of the Defense of Marriage Act (DOMA), which was enacted by President Clinton on September 21, 1996. The act limited marriage to one man and one woman, and denied many federal rights and benefits to same-sex couples. The Windsor case struck down DOMA on June 26, 2013.

Same-sex marriage would become legal across the United States on June 26, 2015, with all married couples being granted the same rights and benefits, following the *Obergefell v. Hodges* Supreme Court decision. Similar to the Windsor case, this case centered on the rights of surviving same-sex spouses. Unable to wed in their home state of Ohio, Jim Obergefell and John Arthur travelled to Maryland to marry. Their marriage wasn't recognized in Ohio, and the pair sued. The case eventually made its way to the Supreme Court. Following the ruling, Obergefell addressed a crowd gathered outside the court, saying in a statement shared by NPR the day of the ruling:

> *I know in my heart that John is with me today. That man cared for and loved me for 21 years through thick and thin. Today's ruling from the Supreme Court affirms what millions across this country already know to be true in our hearts—our love is equal.*

The *Obergefell* ruling also benefited transgender spouses, as the HRC, explained:

> *Because of the Supreme Court's ruling, states may no longer restrict marriage based on gender. This means that whatever your gender, and regardless of whether state officials recognized your gender, this should not affect your ability to marry.*

Since becoming legal, thousands of same-sex couples have taken advantage of their ability to be legally married. According to 2016 census data from Statistics Canada, there were 24,370 couples

CIVIL UNIONS AND DOMESTIC PARTNERSHIPS

Prior to marriage rights being granted to same-sex couples across the United States through the 2015 *Obergefell v. Hodges* Supreme Court decision, civil unions and domestic partnerships were the options available to same-sex couples in some cities and states who wanted legal recognition of their relationships. Domestic partnerships were

(continued on the next page)

(continued from the previous page)

first recognized in Berkeley, California, in 1984. Vermont granted the first civil union in 2000. Six states and the District of Columbia would eventually offer domestic partnerships, while nine states offered civil unions.

There were differences, though, between the benefits and protections provided by these legal relationships and those provided by marriage. Under civil unions and domestic partnerships, same-sex couples were granted many of the same benefits and protections as married couples on the state level. These relationships, though, weren't recognized on the federal level and wouldn't be recognized in all states, either. Some employers would offer partner benefits to their workers. Like marriages, these legal partnerships could be dissolved.

With same-sex marriage now legal across the country, some states have phased out civil unions and domestic partnerships. Some employers that had been offering partner benefits have replaced those with spousal benefits. Civil unions in some states may have been converted into marriages following the *Obergefell* decision, but domestic partnerships may not have been. Therefore, couples would need to marry to keep the benefits they'd enjoyed to this point and have access to more.

in same-sex marriages in the country, compared with 6,449,632 couples in opposite-sex marriages. Data released by the US Census Bureau in 2017, found there were four hundred thousand same-sex married couples and fifty-six million opposite-sex married couples in the country.

BEING A FAMILY

Even with marriage rights, LGBTQ+ people don't necessarily enjoy equal family rights. If same-sex

Same-sex couples have fought for the same parental rights with biological, adopted, and foster children that opposite-sex parents enjoy.

couples adopt or have biological children, both spouses may not have the same parental rights. As a result, same-sex parents may have to go through timely, and costly, processes to enjoy the same parental rights as opposite-sex couples.

One example experienced by same-sex parents in Canada and the United States is people who used a surrogate, egg, or sperm donor to conceive needing to adopt their own children, even if both spouses' names appear on the baby's birth certificate. In Ontario, activism from parents led to the introduction and passage of the All Families Are Equal Act, assented on December 5, 2016. Under the law, legal parental recognition would be granted to same-sex parents in these cases. Following the introduction of the act, Ontario attorney general Yasir Naqvi told the Huffington Post:

> It makes sure that all parents and their children are recognized equally in the law, that there are no extra steps or burdens for parents to go through in order to be declared or recognized as the parent of their child.

Without these protections, parents may have no legal connection to their children if something happened to their spouse or if their relationship ended. Martha and Meredith Holley-Miers of

Washington, DC, have two children together, one Martha gave birth to and the other Meredith gave birth to. Though married, they've each had to go through the process of adopting their children. Meredith shared the concerns she and her wife had for an NPR story:

> *Meredith would be left taking care of a baby that she had no legal bond to. And so if my family decided that they didn't like that, they could take Meredith to court and they would have a stronger legal relationship to our baby than Meredith would if we didn't do the second-parent adoption. Or if we ever—God forbid—were to split up and she didn't have a legal connection to the baby then custody issues would be very difficult for her to pursue a legal custody relationship with the baby.*

For same-sex couples and individuals interested in adopting or fostering other children, there are no legal restrictions. The adoptive and fostering rights of same-sex couples and individuals in the United States depends on where they live. On April 21, 2016, a federal judge struck down a ban in the state of Mississippi on same-sex couples adopting, which made same-sex adoption legal in all fifty states. On February 23, 2018, however, the Georgia Senate passed SB 375, a bill allowing child welfare organizations to discriminate against prospective parents. This included LBGTQ couples, single parents, and inter-faith couples, based on the organization's religious beliefs. Boycotts had been threatened against the state as a result of the bill's passage. Groups including the HRC are advocating for the bill's defeat, as Marty Rouse, HRC national field director, explains:

> Plain and simple—SB 375 is discrimination dressed up as a "solution'" to a fake problem. It creates an unnecessary hardship for potential LGBTQ adoptive or foster parents in Georgia and primarily harms the children

Activists organized to fight implementation of SB 375, a Georgia law that would legalize discrimination by foster and adoption agencies against LGBTQ+ couples and others.

*looking for a loving home. It's unfortunate
that leaders are focusing on this bill, instead
of concrete ways to improve the child welfare system in Georgia. We ask the Georgia
House of Representatives to reject this bill.*

The bill was stripped of its anti-LGBTQ+ provision
before it was passed, but the struggle was far from
over. In July 2018, Robert Aderholt, a Republican
congressman for Alabama, proposed an amend-
ment that would allow federally funded adoption and
foster agencies to reject hopeful parents on the basis
of sexual orientation and religion. States that did not
comply could lose 15 percent of federal funding for
their child welfare services.

Nancy Pelosi, the House Minority Leader, stated
that Republicans "chose to sacrifice the well-be-
ing of little children to push a bigoted, anti-LGBTQ
agenda, potentially denying tens of thousands of
vulnerable children the opportunity to find a loving and safe home... There is no place for bigotry
or discrimination in our foster and adoption sys-
tems—or in any part of our democracy."

Despite the progress that's been made for
LGBTQ+ civil rights, as the passing of this bill and
the fight to repeal it show, the struggle for equality
continues. Through the hard work of advocates
and allies, the goal of equality will be reached.

TIMELINE

1969 Police raid the Stonewall Inn, a bar in New York City with an LGBTQ+ clientele, on June 28.

1970 Activists mark the one-year anniversary of the Stonewall protests with a gay liberation march on June 28 in New York City.

1981 Police in Toronto raid bathhouses in the city, arresting hundreds on February 5.

The New York Times publishes an article on June 3 describing a rare form of cancer diagnosed in gay men in California and New York.

1982 The Centers for Disease Control and Prevention first uses the term "acquired immune deficiency syndrome" (AIDS) on September 24.

1993 President Bill Clinton announces the "Don't Ask, Don't Tell" policy, which prohibits out LGBTQ+ people from serving in the US military, on July 19.

1996 The Canadian Human Rights Act is amended to include sexual orientation as a prohibited ground for discrimination via passage of Bill C-33 on June 20.

President Clinton signs the Defense of Marriage Act (DOMA) into law, limiting the definition of marriage to one man and one woman, on September 21.

2000 Same-sex couples in Canada are granted the same social and tax benefits as

opposite-sex couples in common-law relationships via Bill C-23, assented on June 29.

2005 Same-sex marriage is legalized in Canada
via Bill C-38 on July 20.

2011 The US military's "Don't Ask, Don't Tell" policy is formally repealed on September 20.

2013 DOMA is struck down by the Supreme
Court's ruling in *United States v. Windsor* on
June 26.

2015 Same-sex marriage is legalized in the
United States through the Supreme Court's ruling in *Obergefell v. Hodges* on June 26.

2017 On January 9, US Secretary of State John
Kerry issues an apology to LGBTQ+ workers
for discrimination by the State Department.

The Canadian Human Rights Act is amended
to include gender identity and gender expression as prohibited grounds of discrimination
through passage of Bill C-16 on June 19.

On November 28, Canadian Prime Minister
Justin Trudeau apologizes to LGBTQ+ people
for workplace discrimination by the government
and armed forces.

GLOSSARY

adultery Having sex with someone other than your spouse or partner.

appeal When a higher court is asked to review a lower court's decision.

aversion therapy A treatment that attempts to rid a patient of an undesirable behavior by associating it with something unpleasant.

bisexual A person who can be physically, romantically, or emotionally attracted to people of the same or opposite sex.

boycott Refusing to interact with a business, organization, or person to protest their actions or policies.

curriculum Courses taught and subjects covered in school.

discharge To be released from military service.

electroshock therapy Electrical currents that are passed through the brain to treat mental illness.

exclusionary Rules, laws, or policies that are restrictive.

gay A person who is attracted to people of the same sex, most often describing men who are attracted to other men.

gender Personal identity that may or may not match with the female or male sex someone was assigned at birth.

heterosexual Someone who is attracted to people of the opposite sex.

homophobic A fear of people who are attracted

to the same sex; also used to describe people who are prejudiced or intolerant toward LGBTQ+ people.

homosexual Once commonly used, this outdated term refers to people attracted to people of the same sex.

inclusive Open to or including everyone.

injunction A court order requiring that a particular action be stopped.

lesbian A woman who is attracted to other women.

lobotomy A once-popular surgical procedure that severed nerve tracts in the frontal lobe of the brain to treat mental disorders.

prohibition The act of making something illegal.

repeal To do away with an existing law.

sex The classification of a person as male or female at birth based on bodily characteristics.

sexual orientation A description of a person's attraction to other people.

transgender A person whose gender identity or gender expression differs from the sex they were assigned at birth.

FOR MORE INFORMATION

American Civil Liberties Association (ACLU)
125 Broad Street, 18th Floor
New York, NY 10004
(212) 549-2500
Website: https://www.aclu.org
Facebook and Twitter: @aclu
YouTube: aclu
The ACLU advocates for the constitutionally guaranteed and legally protected individual rights of Americans in the courts, in legislation, and in communities across the United States and Puerto Rico.

Canadian Civil Liberties Association (CCLA)
90 Eglinton Avenue E, Suite 900
Toronto, ON M4P 2Y3
Canada
(416) 363-0321
Website: https://ccla.org
Facebook and Twitter: @cancivlib
YouTube: CanCivLib
The CCLA fights for the constitutionally guaranteed rights and freedoms of Canadians in the courts, in legislation, and in communities across the country.

Egale Canada Human Rights Trust
185 Carlton Street
Toronto, ON M5A 2K7

Canada
(888) 204-7777
Website: http://egale.ca
Facebook, Instagram, and Twitter: @EgaleCanada
YouTube: Egale Canada Human Rights Trust
Egale works to rid the world of anti-LGBTQ bias
    and discrimination through its educational pro-
    grams, outreach efforts, and research.

GLSEN
110 William Street, 30th Floor
New York, NY 10038
(212) 727-0135
Email: info@glsen.org
Website: https://www.glsen.org
Facebook and Twitter: @GLSEN
Instagram: @glsenofficial
YouTube: glsen
GLSEN works with legislators and educators to
    ensure all LGBTQ+ students attend safe and
    affirming schools.

Human Rights Campaign (HRC)
1640 Rhode Island Avenue NW
Washington, DC 20036-3278
(202) 628-4160
Website: http://www.hrc.org
Facebook and Instagram: @humanrightscampaign
Twitter: @HRC

HRC advocates for LGBTQ+ rights and equality, and fights against discrimination.

Lambda Legal
120 Wall Street, 19th Floor
New York, NY 10005-3919
(212) 809-8585
Website: http://www.lambdalegal.org
Facebook and Instagram: @lambdalegal
Twitter: @LambdaLegal
YouTube: lambdalegal
Lambda Legal uses litigation, education, and public policy work to advocate for the full civil rights of LGBTQ+ people.

Lesbian Gay Bi Trans (LGBT) Youth Line
PO Box 73118, Wood Street P.O.
Toronto, ON M4Y 2W5
Canada
(800) 268-9688
Website: http://www.youthline.ca
Facebook and Instagram: @lgbtyouthline
Twitter: @LGBTYouthLine
YouTube: lgbtyouthline
LGBT Youth Line provides anonymous peer support and referrals to LGBTQ+ teens and young adults through its telephone, chat, and text services.

Grinapol, Corinne. *Harvey Milk: Pioneering Gay Politician* (Remarkable LGBTQ Lives). New York, NY: Rosen Publishing, 2015.

Heitkamp, Kristina Lyn. *Gay-Straight Alliances: Networking with Other Teens and Allies* (The LGBTQ+ Guide to Beating Bullying). New York, NY: Rosen Publishing, 2018.

Hurt, Avery Elizabeth. *Confronting LGBTQ+ Discrimination* (Speak Up! Confronting Discrimination in Your Daily Life). New York, NY: Rosen Publishing, 2018.

Hurt, Avery Elizabeth. *Coping with Hate and Intolerance* (Coping). New York, NY: Rosen Publishing, 2018.

Hurt, Avery Elizabeth. *Working with Your School to Create a Safe Environment* (The LGBTQ+ Guide to Beating Bullying). New York, NY: Rosen Publishing, 2018.

Jennings, Jazz. *Being Jazz: My Life as a (Transgender) Teen*. New York, NY: Ember, 2016.

Koya, Lena, and Alexandra Hanson-Harding. *Female Activists* (Women in the World). New York, NY: Rosen Publishing, 2018.

Landau, Jennifer. *Teens Talk About Leadership and Activism* (Teen Voices: Real Teens Discuss Real Problems). New York, NY: Rosen Publishing, 2018.

Landau, Jennifer. *Teens Talk About Suicide, Death, and Grieving* (Teen Voices: Real Teens Discuss

Real Problems). New York, NY: Rosen Publishing, 2018.

Penne, Barbara. *Your Rights as an LGBTQ+ Teen* (The LGBT+ Guide to Beating Bullying). New York, NY: Rosen Publishing, 2017.

Prager, Sarah. *Queer, There, and Everywhere: 23 People Who Changed the World.* New York, NY: HarperCollins Children's Books, 2017.

Staley, Erin. *Laverne Cox* (Transgender Pioneers). New York, NY: Rosen Publishing, 2017.

BIBLIOGRAPHY

All Things Considered. "Obama on Same-Sex Marriage Ruling: We've Made U.S. 'A Little More Perfect.'" NPR, June 26, 2015. https://www.npr.org/2015/06/26/417840285/obama-on-same-sex-marriage-ruling-weve-made-u-s-a-little-more-perfect.

All Things Considered. "Same-Sex Spouses Turn to Adoption to Protect Parental Rights." NPR, September 22, 2017. https://www.npr.org/2017/09/22/551814731/same-sex-spouses-turn-to-adoption-to-protect-parental-rights.

Altman, Lawrence K. "Rare Cancer Seen in 41 Homosexuals." *New York Times*, July 3, 1981. https://www.nytimes.com/1981/07/03/us/rare-cancer-seen-in-41-homosexuals.html.

American Experience: Stonewall Uprising. PBS, April 25, 2011.

The Battle of amfAR. Directed by Rob Epstein and Jeffrey Friedman. HBO, 2013.

Bridges, Alicia. "Inclusive Curriculum Part of Discussion at Gathering of LGBT School Groups." CBC News, November 20, 2017. http://www.cbc.ca/news/canada/saskatoon/lgbt-gsa-summit-saskatchewan-saskatoon-1.4409685.

CBS Reports: The Homosexuals. CBS, March 7, 1967.

Dawson, Peter. "Transgender Wrestler Mack Beggs Is Booed After Second Straight State Title Win." *Star-Telegram*, February 24, 2018.

http://www.star-telegram.com/sports
/article202001904.html.

Gutowitz, Jill. "Coming Out at Work Is Way More
Complicated Than You Think." *Vice*, November
3, 2017. https://www.vice.com/en_ca/article
/evba8k/coming-out-at-work-is-more
-complicated-than-you-think.

How to Survive a Plague. Directed by David
France. Sundance Selects, 2012.

Ibbitson, John. "How Michelle Douglas Broke
Down the Canadian Military's LGBT Walls."
Globe and Mail, October 23, 2017. https://www
.theglobeandmail.com/news/politics
/interrogation-dismissal-and-now-an-apology
-to-michelle-douglas/article36700166.

Jones, Allison. "Same-Sex Parents in Ontario No
Longer Have to Adopt Their Own Kids." Huffington Post, October 1, 2016. http://www
.huffingtonpost.ca/2016/10/01/all-families-are
-equal-ac_n_12285612.html.

MacLean, Cameron. "LGBT Families File Human
Rights Complaints Over School Curriculum."
CBC News, June 23, 2017. http://www.cbc.ca
/news/canada/manitoba/lgbt-human-rights
-school-curriculum-1.4175636.

Musto, Michael. "Why Don't Gays and Lesbians
Get Along Better?" Out.com, June 30, 2014.
https://www.out.com/entertainment/michael
-musto/2014/06/30/why-don%E2%80%99t.

-gays-and-lesbians-get-along-better.

Nasser, Shanifa. "Gay Activist Files Complaint Over Blood-Donation Waiting Period." CBC, August 26, 2016. http://www.cbc.ca/news /canada/toronto/gay-activist-files-federal -human-rights-complaint-over-blood-donation -wait-period-1.3738029.

Silva, Christianna. "Schools Won't Teach Children About Lesbian Sex and That's Hurting Queer Girls." *Newsweek*, January 19, 2018. http:// www.newsweek.com/sex-education-failing -everyone-especially-queer-women-704715.

Swardson, Anne. "Gay Couple Test Canadian Tolerance/Longtime Lovers Fight a Legal Battle for Spousal Benefits." *Washington Post*, January 4, 1995. https://www.sfgate.com/news/article /Gay-Couple-Test-Canadian-Tolerance -Longtime-3049800.php.

Talk of the Nation. "What Changes After Supreme Court Rulings on Prop 8 and DOMA." NPR, June 26, 2013. https://www.npr.org.

Taylor, Jessica. "Rise Of LGBTQ Candidates Could Usher In A 'Rainbow Wave' In 2018." Morning Edition, September 3, 2018. www.npr.org.

The Trans List. Directed by Timothy Greenfield-Sanders. HBO, 2016.

WTF with Marc Maron. Episode 422 with Dan Savage, September 9, 2013.

INDEX

ABOUT THE AUTHOR

Devlin Smith has been writing about topics ranging from pop culture to small businesses to home décor for nearly two decades. She was inspired to study journalism by a desire to connect people and share their stories, earning a bachelor's degree from Chapman University. Smith's first published piece was an essay about the death of AIDS activist and reality television star Pedro Zamora for her local newspaper when she was in high school. Today, she works as a creative copywriter for the University of California, Riverside, where she writes for departments across campus, including the university's Ethnic & Gender Programs.

PHOTO CREDITS